A SINGLE MOMS
SURVIVAL GUIDE
A Story of Forgiving Giving and Blessing

MAUREEN A BRUNDAGE

Copyright © 2015 by Maureen A Brundage

A Single Moms Survival Guide
A Story of Forgiving Giving and Blessing
by Maureen A Brundage

Printed in the United States of America.
Edited by Xulon Press.

ISBN 9781498454315

All rights reserved solely by the author. The author guarantees all contents are original and do not infringe upon the legal rights of any other person or work. No part of this book may be reproduced in any form without the permission of the author. The views expressed in this book are not necessarily those of the publisher.

Scripture quotations taken from the English Standard Version (ESV). Copyright © 2001 by Crossway, a publishing ministry of Good News Publishers. Used by permission. All rights reserved.

www.xulonpress.com

Table of Contents

Chapter 1 7

Chapter 2 11

Chapter 3 17

Chapter 4 21

Chapter 5 25

Chapter 6 29

Conclusion 35

CHAPTER 1

I stood in the bedroom as he said to me, "I can't take the responsibility anymore."

I thought he referred to the groceries we were responsible for in our community living. I said, "That's okay; I can do the shopping."

He said, "No, I mean, I don't want this responsibility. I wish I could move away and start all over again."

"It's okay. We can move away."

"No. I mean I want to move away without you."

As the words sunk in, I went numb. I was pregnant with our fourth son. At that moment, my life became a nightmare of pain I never realized possible. It was at one point I decided it would be best to take some pills and end it. It was me he didn't want. I felt as though someone had tied my hands behind my back and stuck a knife in my heart I couldn't pull out.

It was a rainy night. He hadn't moved out yet. I couldn't sleep and the pain had blinded me. I went outside at 1:30 a.m. to walk the country road on which we lived. It was pouring rain. The rain was so loud that it drowned out my sobbing.

I was soaked and climbed into our sixteen-foot travel trailer and lay down, shaking and crying uncontrollably. I couldn't catch my breath. I knew what I was going to do the next day.

As I lay there I cried out to God, "God, I know you are real. Please be more real to me now than you have ever been."

It was at that point I heard plainly, "Thou shall not kill." It shook me out of my clouded reality that I would not only end my life, but the life of my baby. A peace came over me. I got up realizing the pain was still intense, but I had to go on.

So began a journey I would never have planned or chosen, with many miracles of God's faithfulness and love. In spite of my failures, He was faithful. When nothing made sense, He loved me.

As I began the long trip on the train to Utah with the boys, I was numb. It was a trip we were supposed to take as a family in the car. I knew what I would face when I returned. I knew at that point I had to be strong and happy for my little ones. I was seven months pregnant. My oldest had recently turned four, my second son would turn three on this trip, and the baby was eighteen months old.

I spent the next two weeks with my parents and my favorite aunt from Maryland. I dreaded telling my parents. I wanted to keep things happy for my family. I finally told my dad at about 11:30 p.m. He and my mom were packing to leave with my aunt to go to Maryland at 6:30 a.m. As I gave my dad the news I would face when I got home, he looked up at me and started yelling for my mom. I was scared. The words are all blurred in my mind. I began to cry as my parents and aunt realized my world had crumbled and there was nothing they could do.

Chapter 1

I faced my dad and said, "Daddy, I love him and I am forgiving him. Please don't say anything bad about him in front of the boys."

I remember standing at the foot of the bed my brother sat on, repeating those words. As I said them, I also was in disbelief this had happened. After my parents left, I stayed a few days longer. Before I left, I learned there was a strike with the engineers of the trains. We were delayed at least another week. How ironic I would return on our fifth anniversary.

The train ride home was dreadful. I couldn't believe when I returned, he would be gone, so I prayed. I remember on the train ride home we were in a car with retired schoolteachers from the Midwest. They were amazed at how well Michael could color and print his name. They read to the boys. James charmed them with his smile. The boys didn't have a clue daddy would be gone when they got home. The people were so loving and caring, it was almost as if they sensed something was wrong in our lives. They were God's angels to me. They held the boys as they took naps and made them laugh.

Chapter 2

Choosing to forgive no matter what was something I had locked in my heart. I could not have done this without the strength of the Lord. I had seen divorce rip families. I had seen what un-forgiveness had done to people. I never dreamed my choice would speak volumes to my dad. One of the criteria for choosing to forgive is locking into it at every chance. "God, I don't feel like it." "God, this hurts." "God, this doesn't make sense." "God, this isn't fair. What do I get out of it?"

The other criterion for choosing to forgive was to raise the kids to love their dad and not allow them to hear me or anyone else say anything bad about him. They loved their dad. I realized and had seen my sons were part of each of us. If I were to put him down in front of the boys, I would hurt their self-image.

I was about to set out on one of the most difficult journeys of my life, but also one that held the most miracles.

As I put the boys down for their nap, I went into my room, got on my knees, and prayed. As I prayed one day, the Lord gave me the name Phillip. He spoke clearly about this child. People who loved me surrounded me. My friends were there to help me every step of the way. They were my angels. On November 18, 1978, my fourth son, Phillip was born.

The day he arrived my sister and dear friends surrounded me. My sister Clare had taken time out of her busy schedule to come be with me. As soon as he was born, my friend held him up for me to see.

I said, "That is Phillip," and as I said that, he turned his little head with eyes wide open and looked directly at me. I find it amazing the Lord gave me his name, which means, "lover of horses," when my sister Clare has always loved horses.

The night of November 18, it snowed. I was amazed and excited God would do that for us. I loved snow; it comforted my heart. It was as if the Lord had said, "Here is my gift to you." I felt so loved by Him even in the midst of my heartbreak. I felt His favor on my son.

There were many of God's little miracles. It felt like at night, after the boys were down, I fed and rocked Phillip. Many nights I held him and cried. Phil looked up and smiled even before the normal age for smiling. It was as if he said to me, "It's okay, Mom." I felt the Lord comfort my heart through his little smiles.

My parents had sent me some money for Christmas. On Christmas Eve, I went to Mr. Steak with the three older boys. As I sat in the restaurant, my son James sat in the high chair on the end of the table. He was twenty-two months at the time. He turned his head and smiled sweetly at someone behind me. He giggled and turned back. Before we finished, a man walked by and put a dollar in his hand. He said, "His smile just made my Christmas," and walked out. I realized how lonely that man must have felt.

Chapter 2

The house where we had lived with another family had sold. I did not feel good about the move to the community farm. I realized I would have to live in a sixteen-foot travel trailer with my four sons. My other choice at that time was government housing in Portland—not a good one at the time.

One Wednesday before Easter, we were notified we had to be out by Saturday. I sat at the dinner table and reality hit me. I felt overwhelmed and hopeless. I ran upstairs and threw myself on the bed and sobbed. I was a scared twenty-six-year-old with four babies. Where would I go? I had no car. I didn't want to raise our sons in the drug-infested government housing. I lay there crying uncontrollably. Crying to God to help me, "What should I do?"

I felt this overwhelming peace come over me. As I lay there, I saw a picture in my head of a lush green valley with beautiful rolling hills on each side. A shepherd walked with a herd of sheep. In the middle of the herd, one sheep kicked his hooves up, *baaing* and *baaing*, scared of where he was.

The Lord said to me clearly, "That is you. I have you right in the middle of my people and right in the middle of my will and I will take care of you."

I laid there in total peace. I said, "Okay Lord, you are going to show me how to pack. I don't know where I am going." I could not deny the peace. I was not afraid. I knew God had a plan.

On Friday morning, I got a call from a friend and she asked me if I was ready for some good news. I said, "Yes."

She said Ina had been praying for me and wanted to know how I was doing. When my friend told her, she said it just so happened she and her sister were coming to bring her sister's foster daughter to visit her dad for spring break. She wanted the boys and me to come back with her. Amazingly, I had packed two suitcases and three boxes. One was full of cloth diapers for two of my babies. I didn't have much—three cribs, my dresser, and one dresser for the boys—that went into storage on the farm.

I had met Ina as she had come to stay with us three and a half years earlier. She was like a mother to me. She had delivered my son John when he was born. She lived eight hours away in McKinleyville, California. I had been there one other time and all I remembered was the fog and rain. I figured I would be back to Portland in two months. I thought I would heal and come right back.

So my journey started. I arrived in McKinleyville on a foggy misty Easter Sunday night in 1979. My sons were four, three, two, and five months old. I had no car and no home. I didn't know where my life was going.

This began a lesson in trusting God for everything. There was no better teacher than Ina. She knew the Lord and His Word. She and her sister Nita began to help me raise my sons. We went to church every time the doors were open. I figured I would go back to Portland soon. Knowing I had no money, I had to trust the Lord for every penny. Ina and Nita went out of their way to make sure we felt at home by cooking great meals and letting the boys help with little chores. They loved my boys. Taking us in had a huge impact on my life and my sons.

After only being there a week, there was a knock on the door. I opened the door and found a UPS man with a box for us. As he handed me the box, I thanked him and said they were Easter treats from my Mother. I was so happy to hear one of the first people I met talk about Jesus. He began to tell me of how the Lord had healed him of Sarcodosis. He never knew how that simple conversation would set my faith for a healing in my life and also a connection to an awesome Christian family.

Ina began to teach me tithing and giving. One day a lady came to Ina's door. She had a little boy with her. She said she needed money for gas and food. Since Ina's house was next to a church, many people thought it was the pastor's home. My heart broke for her. I was ready to give her every last penny.

Ina took me aside and said, "I know she does this to get money for drugs. You may go to the store and buy her food and put gas in her tank, but do not give her money." She quoted a scripture I had never heard, but would stay with me forever: "I have not seen the righteous forsaken or His seed begging bread." I knew if I put Him first, He would provide.

CHAPTER 3

I lived with Ina for three months. She and Nita watched the boys in their beauty shop while I cleaned houses. I was so thankful for Ina's praying with me and loving the boys. She taught me how to raise the boys. After three months, Ina's husband Bob came home from Detroit. He had been attending a mechanics school. It was time to move on. Nita said she wanted me with her and she didn't feel it was time for me to go out on my own.

The last night at Ina's, I stayed and cleaned. I had taken the boys over to Nita's around the block. I finished cleaning close to midnight. As I finished, the overwhelming feeling of not having a place to call home hit me. I knelt down by Ina's bed and cried again, "Lord I don't have my own home. I've lived with other people, where is my life going?"

Again I heard so clearly, "My daughter, it is my good pleasure to give you the kingdom" (Luke 12:32).

I got up walked around the corner to Nita's home. At that time, it was after midnight. I sat on her couch opened her big family Bible and my eyes fell on, "Foxes have holes, the birds of the air have nests, but the Son of man has no place to lay his head" (Matthew 8:20).

I prayed and told the Lord I knew He would provide for the boys and me even if He sent us into the mission field in tents. I held tightly to the scripture that says, "He is a Father to the fatherless and a husband to the widow" (Psalm 68:5). I realized I had to trust Him for everything, so I began to tithe sixty dollars a month. One of the first real challenges I had in my faith was when I went to a meeting and the Lord laid it on my heart to give the one hundred dollar bill I had. It was scary, but I knew it was the Lord.

Three months later, someone walked up to me and put five hundred dollars in my hand.

The Lord provided my home. Nita had the boys and I live with her for a year. She offered her house to the new pastor coming from Australia, so I began to look for a home. I knew the Lord had my home. Every call I made, I was asked what my husband did.

I responded with, "I'm a single mother."

They asked what I did for a living and I said, "Clean houses and babysit."

Their next question was, "How many children do you have?"

I said, "I have four sons."

Everyone told me, "No thank you," and hung up.

I got to the point of saying, "I'd like to look at your home. I am a single mom with four sons and I have a cleaning business."

I kept praying. I knew God had my home. *He* was my provider and loved the boys and I more than anyone. One day I called a lady and told her my situation. She said she

Chapter 3

had been a single mom with three girls. She encouraged me to come by and look at the home. I entered to find the house full of interested people. To my amazement, she picked me. I was so fortunate to live surrounded by such caring neighbors. She was an amazing landlady.

The Lord cared about every area of my life. I found myself sixty dollars short of my past-due rent. Ina's family and friends came to visit and were camping at Clam Beach. It was a drizzly and foggy fall night. I invited them all to stay with the boys and me because I had plenty of floor space and beds, which was better than a tent on the cold beach. We were up late talking about the Lord and His miracles. The next morning before they left, we all joined hands and prayed. After we were finished, one of the sons gave me what I thought was a five-dollar bill. I put it on the counter and left to take the boys to school. When I got home I looked and it was three twenty-dollar bills. Amazing how the Lord provided exactly what I needed.

I was eighty-five dollars behind on my Christian school tuition. I stood in my bedroom again and cried out to the Lord. What could I do? I felt a gentle voice urging me to write a letter. In my bedroom was a dresser I had in Oregon. It was a heavy, dark, Mediterranean dresser. The handles were broken on it and it was a pain to try to open. I knew I had stationery in there I never used. At this prompting, I wrestled the handles to open the drawer. I reached into a stack of envelopes of stationery and pulled out a thin box. I opened it and I saw some money inside the box. I was so shocked I could hardly breathe, as I counted four twenty-dollar bills and one five-dollar bill. I *hit the floor*! In His presence, I could not move.

Chapter 4

I loved my home. I wanted to take care of it. The scripture says, "He that is faithful in little will be entrusted with much" (Luke 16:10). I knew even though I rented, I had to treat my home as if I owned it. I wanted to be an example to my boys and to teach them we were to be good stewards of what He has given us.

I loved my neighborhood. I cleaned houses and babysat. I was fortunate enough to receive housing authority. This allowed me to put my boys in Arcata Christian School. What a blessing to have a principal that was not only a godly man, but had a sense of humor. My boys loved him.

I cleaned houses during the day. After the boys and I were home, I would put my little guy Phillip in my backpack and with Mike, John, and James and go through the forest to McKinleyville High School. I would put Phil in the sandpit and tell his brothers to watch him as I ran the track.

My first car was a little yellow Gremlin. My friend wanted to sell her Gremlin for $700, but the Lord told her to sell it to me for $350. However, there was only one problem: I didn't have $350. Within a couple of days, the parents of a boy whom I babysat said they had prayed and they felt they were supposed to loan me the money for a new car. God is faithful.

One October Friday night, I babysat my friend's daughter. As we went outside, I felt a strange stillness in the air. I remember thinking as I looked at the full moon, "This is earthquake weather." Since I had never experienced an earthquake before, it was odd I was able to sense one coming.

The boys were asleep and we had to be up early so I could get them to Ina and Nita's beauty shop and go to work cleaning houses.

I fell asleep and dreamt it was the end of the world and no one was around. It was a weird feeling. The stillness in the dream was unbearable. All of a sudden, I woke up to my bed shaking back and forth. It was an old antique bed with wheels on the frame. The chandelier over the kitchen table shook like crazy. I could hear the handles on my boys bed clanking. I froze, terrified. My son John had crawled into my bed and soundly slept.

My son Mike screamed, "Mommy!"

I said, "Get in here." I listened for anything from Phil or James' room. I began to say, "God hasn't given me a spirit of fear, but of love, of power, and a sound mind" (2 Timothy 1:7). God gives His angels charge over us to keep us in all our ways (Psalm 91:11).

My son Mike said, "Is my daddy okay?"

The Portland area had experienced the Mount St. Helens Volcano. We had been there that summer. I told him his daddy was fine. As I quoted the scriptures, a peace came over me. He gives His angels charge over me to keep me in all my ways.

As I started to fall asleep, I heard a wind come up. My home bordered the schoolyard and when the wind blew, it made a whirling wind sound through the picket fence. The

Chapter 4

bush by my window blew back and forth and scratched my window. I thought, *how strange an earthquake could stir up the atmosphere and the wind could blow this hard.* Since I had never been in one, I didn't know what to expect.

Later that afternoon, I got home. I talked to a neighbor about the earthquake. I commented that I thought it was strange a wind came up after the earthquake. She looked at me and said, "There was *no* wind. It was still."

I said, "How late were you up?"

She said she had been up until 5:30. I knew I had fallen asleep before that. In fact, I fell asleep to the wind. So I decided to check with my neighbor down the street. I called and asked if she thought it strange that there was a strong wind after the earthquake.

She also said, "There was *no* wind. It was still."

I again asked how late she was up and she said until 5:30 also.

I knew I didn't imagine it because the bush scratched my window. The sound of the wind blew through my fence. It was at that point I realized God gave His angels charge over me. I had never had God show Himself so real.

I was fortunate to have Pastor Col Stringer and his beautiful wife, Jan in my life. They had packed up their family of four and came to pastor a tiny church in McKinleyville from Australia. Their teaching was strong on the Word of God and His promises. Both Col and Jan were fun to be around. His stories of big game hunting in Australia were entertaining. He was a real-life Crocodile Dundee. He had a way of teaching the Word of God and relating it to our everyday lives.

The boys and I were at church Sunday mornings and evenings and Wednesday nights with Ina and Nita. One service I was in the back of the church crying. I was overwhelmed with all I had to do. I prayed, "Lord I forgive my ex-husband. I forgive his friend."

The Lord spoke clearly to me and said, "You have forgiven them. You haven't forgiven Me."

I was stunned. I realized deep in my heart, I had this expectation that because my first husband had led me to the Lord and we had these beautiful children, my life would be happy and perfect. When I gave my life to the Lord, I experienced a 180-degree turn. When my husband left, my life crumbled. I never realized I judged God for this. How could I do that? Still, God knew. Who has to forgive God? He's perfect. I realized it was a judgment in my heart. I said, "God, I forgive you." It felt weird, but there was a sense of relief.

Chapter 5

As I decorated my Christmas tree, I felt overwhelmed with sadness. The rest of my family would be together in Utah for Christmas, but I could not afford to go. I decorated my tree, which had been given to me. As I picked up one of the Christmas balls, I looked at it and made the decision to be thankful for it. I began to say, "Thank you God for this." As I picked up the next one I said, "Thank you God for this one too." I picked up the next and said, "Thank you God for this one and thank you for my beautiful tree." It was at that point I could hear my boys playing in the back room. I said, "Thank you God, for Mike, John, James, and Phil."

It was as if the floodgates opened. I began to thank the Lord for everything I could think of: my home, my family, and amazingly, my sadness left. My whole mood changed from sad to joyful. I appreciated what I had, rather than feeling sad for what I didn't have. However, what was even more amazing was what was about to unfold.

I was dedicated to tithing, despite my sparse income. I brought in six hundred dollars a month so ten percent tithing would be sixty dollars a month. There was only one problem: all I had for Christmas presents for my four sons was twenty dollars. That's five dollars per boy. The Lord had made a way for me to move back into Nita's house and rent it. I was now in a great neighborhood with awesome families.

However, Christmas morning was a difficult one for me. I could not afford the kind of presents for my sons that their friends had. Not only that, but some of the dads were outside with their children playing with their new bikes and toys. My boys had neither. I realized if I didn't tithe, I could take my sixty dollars plus the twenty dollars and have twenty dollars for each boy. It wasn't a lot, but it was better than five dollars per boy.

Should I tithe? God would understand. He knew my struggle. The boys would get a few more gifts. However, God, you said in Malachi, "*Prove Me now* and see if I won't pour out the blessings of heaven" (Malachi 3:10). I thought of my boys on Christmas morning and saw the other kids in the neighborhood. How will they feel? Would I look at the facts or believe God's promise?

I asked my landlord if I could pay half the rent now and half next month. She said no because they had bills to pay on the house. That door was shut. *Okay Lord, You have never let me down before. I am choosing to tithe no matter what. I know you will catch me.*

On Christmas morning, I got a call from my neighbor. She said, "I need you to come over."

I immediately thought, *I can't go there with my boys*, so I told her I couldn't because my family would call and I needed to be home for the call. However, all I could think about was she had her whole family there with awesome gifts for their kids and I was afraid my boys would feel sad.

She said, "If you don't come over, I'm going to come get you." I knew she actually would. So the boys and I went two

Chapter 5

doors down. As we walked through the door, I saw place full of relatives and kids. She asked all five of us to sit on the couch. As we sat down, I looked up and down the hallway came five of her children. In front of us, they placed a bag full of presents for each of us. I started to cry, and when I looked up some of her family was crying too. They didn't even realize the miracle that had just happened. I could hear the excitement as the boys dug into their bags of gifts, "Wow! Look at this!" I never thought the day I chose to put God first and trust Him, it would open the door to so many blessings.

Chapter 6

As a single mom, all of the money I earned or was gifted to me went to my boys. I couldn't even afford the twenty-five-cent ice cream at the drug store. My mother had sent me sixty dollars to use "only on myself." One day, I saw a mannequin in the store dressed in a cute blouse, a beige loose knit sweater, rose jeans, and a pair of brown boots. I looked at it and said, "Lord, you are my husband. I would love to have that outfit. "

One of my friends asked if I could feed her cat while she was on a trip. When she got home, she gave me the exact blouse I had seen on the mannequin. My mother-in-law sent me a package for my birthday, and inside was a loose knit, off-white sweater, similar to the one on the model.

At the time, there was a local shoe store closing. I went in there and found the brown boots I wanted in my size. They were marked down to sixty dollars. I went to the shelf, laid my hands on them, and thanked the Lord they were mine. I prayed for the Lord to "hold" them for me until the price went down, but the store would be closed in a few days. So I went back a few days later and they were twenty dollars and the only pair left on the shelf.

In that same shopping center was an outlet store. I walked in and at the time, Rose Brand jeans were in style. There was no way I could spend a lot of money on them, so I walked over to the clearance table and saw a few blouses and pants. Among them was a pair of those jeans, marked down with an extra percentage off of the lowest price. I tried them on and they were a perfect fit.

When I went to check out, the cashier said, "Where did you find these?" I pointed to the table. She looked at the tag and said, "These shouldn't even be marked down."

Then realized this pair had specifically been marked.

She said, "Well, I need to honor that."

I got a thirty-eight-dollar pair of rose jeans for eight dollars. As I walked out of the store, I realized the Lord had completed my outfit. He loved me. I was His daughter and He delighted in me.

I was fortunate to be able to clean the gym in exchange for my membership. It was there I realized the enjoyment of weightlifting, aerobics, running, and roller-skating. Being there was the only time I had to focus on *me*. I needed to be strong for my boys; I wanted to be a role model for them.

My first friend in Humboldt, Linda, became like a sister to me; she was my prayer partner and someone I knew could always make laugh. We had both felt the Lord wanted us to take the boys to Portland. The boys could see their dad and she and I would visit my friends. As we drove about two hours from home, I realized in my hurry to get all four boys organized and packed, I had left my jacket at home. I prayed, "Oh Lord, please help me find a sweater." I had an extra thirty-five dollars my mom had sent to me. "Just for you," she would say. While we stayed with my friends, I sat on the

Chapter 6

bedroom floor and prayed. I opened my Bible to Malachi 3, which talks about tithing.

Bring the whole tithe to the storehouse that there may be food in my house and prove me now by it, says the Lord of Hosts, if I will not open the windows of Heaven for you and pour you out a blessing that there shall not be room enough to receive it. And I will rebuke the devourer for your sakes and he shall not destroy the fruits of your ground, neither shall your vine drop its fruit before its time in the field, says the Lord of Hosts.

As I read this, I had a feeling the Lord told me to put my whole tithe to my church. Up until that time, I had put my ten percent to my boys' Christian school tuition. Now the Lord took me to the next level. *How can I do that*, I thought. He had already honored my tithe because that was my boys' storehouse. It became clear to me He waited for my answer. I thought, *It's sixty dollars; how can I do that? Lord, you've never let me down.* There was a struggle of my faith in His provision. I call it "falling off the faith cliff"—I don't know where I will land, but I know God will catch me.

So I said, "Yes Lord." I realized I was already behind on my tuition for the month. My brain raced from thought to thought. "Okay Lord; you will have to take this one."

That day my friend and I went to a department store. She wanted some boots. I had prayed when I realized I had forgotten my jacket for God to help me find something cheap to replace that jacket I had forgotten. I had thirty-five dollars for spending. As we walked through the store, I tried to imagine what it would be like to walk into a store like that and buy something. The cashier, distracted, fiddled with the register tape. She finally said, "Go through those curtains to the next department and they will help you."

As we went through to the next department I noticed a table of clothes piled high. I began to look through them. I found a white, loose-knit jacket. It was snuggly and perfect. I looked at the price tag. I was shocked at the discounted price. So I kept digging. I ended up getting a blouse, a gunnysack skirt, and a pair of slacks. As I went to the register to pay, with all the discounts, my total came to just under thirty-three dollars. I was amazed at how God had honored me. As a single mom, I hardly ever spend money on myself. However, this time, I felt the love of the Father say, "I will provide."

The cashier looked at my total and said, "Wow, you are lucky today; $167 of clothes for $32.67."

I said, "It's not luck. God did this for me today."

We soon realized if the register tape hadn't gotten stuck, I wouldn't have been directed through the curtain and found my treasures. God is a loving and faithful Father.

The following Monday I walked into the office of the principal of the boys' school. I said, "Mr. Wunner, I am going to have to pull the boys out of school. I know I am behind on tuition."

He looked at me and said, "I was going to call you and talk to you about that."

I knew it was coming. My heart was sad. The school had such godly men teaching my boys; they needed this. He said, "Someone gave a donation to the school. The school board decided since you had the most children in the school, had been here for a long time, and were a single mom, their tuition is covered."

I was shocked. I flashed back to my struggle with my saying "yes" to the Lord as I prayed. He provided all my new

Chapter 6

clothes. I thanked him as I cried. As I went out the door, there stood our loving school secretary with a smile on her face and tears in her eyes. We hugged. She knew my struggles. She was my rock in a clothing of God's love. (By the way – remember the UPS man who shared God's love and healing when I first moved down? The UPS man was her husband.) God is so good to bless me. *God, how can I doubt you?*

As I prayed one day, the Lord impressed on me to tithe my food stamps. *Tithe my food stamps? Is that you telling me this, Lord?* Our refrigerator was never bare, but it was empty enough at the end of the month that I could wipe it down. I got ninety-two dollars in food stamps each month for the five of us, so roughly ten dollars per person, per month. Nervously, I said yes to what the Lord asked me to do and I bought ten dollars worth of food and gave it to a person in need.

About two weeks later I walked up my porch to find a box full of probably one hundred dollars worth of food, laundry soap, and cleaning supplies. No one knew but the Lord! I got a call at the end of that month. It was a friend's husband. He had just gotten out of jail, and needed food for his family, so I loaded them up with three grocery bags of food and produce.

Conclusion

My dad, my sister, the boys, and I climbed one of my dad's favorite hikes up Logan Canyon, Utah. We got to the top and overlooked the valley. My dad referred back to that late night five years earlier—the night I told him what I would face when I got home. He thought I was crazy to forgive the boys' dad. He then told me about his aunt, who had the same thing happen to her. Only her husband left her with five children. He said she became bitter and angry because of her un-forgiveness.

He told me now that he saw my life, and how well-adjusted and happy the boys and I were, he knew I made the right decision to forgive. That meant the world to me. God had blessed my life.

The fruit of forgiveness is sweet.

www.ingramcontent.com/pod-product-compliance
Lightning Source LLC
LaVergne TN
LVHW021744060526
838200LV00052B/3465